Flowers and Plants in Machine Embroidery

Flowers and Plants in Machine Embroidery

Alison Holt

B.T. Batsford Ltd, London

First published 1990 by
B. T. Batsford Ltd.
583 Fulham Road
London SW6 5BY

Reissued 1997

ISBN 0 7134 6528 X

Printed in China

Photography by Andrea Liggins and John Beynon

CONTENTS

INTRODUCTION

Machine embroidery is a versatile, creative way to interpret a design in colour, line, texture or all three. It offers tremendous scope in variety of technique, texture and scale of working. It has a spontaneity and freshness that hand embroidery often loses because of the time it takes to complete. There is a special thrill to creating a design and executing it in a matter of hours with machine embroidery.

The technique has a vitality which is aided by its particular characteristics. In creating pictures with thread you are mixing together dots of pure colour, formed by small stitches, all lying in different directions, which by catching the light make you aware of the texture. It has similarities with Pointillism and Impressionism, two styles of painting which give tremendous feelings of light, colour and presence because of their technique of small touches of colour. The eye blends the many colours together, but they retain a vibrance, sparkle, and quality not achieved by blending colours in paint in a traditional way. Machine embroidery echoes this quality. As a medium, it has all the potential of painting and more. It can combine techniques with results similar to the subtleties of water-colour painting with the richness of working with oils. Within one piece of work, you can have washes of colour, used for the sky or background, together with detail expressed in various degrees of texture through stitch, which can provide either a fine line, or a wealth of texture or colour. The equivalent would be oil paint laid down with a palette knife. Used in conjunction with quilting, appliqué and lace work, all these combine to make a very exciting medium.

Once you haver mastered the basic skill, the possibilities are endless. One particular appeal of the technique is that not only are results effective at a beginner's level, but that your skills can continue to develop over many years.

1
THE SEWING MACHINE

3 Field of poppies

Creative machine embroidery can be done on any domestic electric sewing machine, but there is scope for a greater variety of stitches if the machine has a swing needle and can therefore do zigzag or satin stitch.

To adapt the machine for embroidery, lower the feed dog, take off the presser foot and stretch some fabric in an embroidery hoop. This is guided underneath the needle, as if you were drawing by moving a piece of paper around under a pencil.

Design variations mean that some machines are easier to adapt for machine embroidery than others. There are a number of computerised and electronic machines available today. Many of their extra features are unnecessary for machine embroidery and some are even restrictive, as if technical advances conflict with creativity. When choosing a machine with embroidery in mind, here are the features to consider.

Stitch width control

This starts at 0 to give a running stitch and increases through to 4 for various widths of zigzag. The control needs to be one that either slides or turns smoothly to give a gradual increase in stitch width. Some machines have push or touch button controls to select stitch width, but this results in the stitch size increasing in steps, and can be rather restrictive when trying to draw using this technique.

Feed dog

This feeds the fabric through the machine at a certain length of stitch in a straight line. For embroidery it needs to be removed to give the freedom to move the work in any direction. Most machines have the facility to drop this feed below the base. A raised plate

which covers the feed, a necessity on some makes of machine, is a poor compromise. It makes the hoop unstable and can restrict the space between the needle and the base of the machine, making it difficult to get the hoop in position under the needle. On machines of this type it is sometimes easier to put the length of stitch control on 0 so that the feed just goes up and down, which interferes with your work less than a raised plate.

Bobbin case

Interesting variations of stitch and texture can be achieved by altering the bobbin tension. It helps if your machine has a removable bobbin case, enabling you to turn the tension screw on the case more easily. Some machines have a self-correcting tension on the bobbin, designed to cope with subtle variations of thickness in the thread, but this feature prevents any control of the bobbin tension. If you are wary of changing the tension, you could buy a spare bobbin case to use just for embroidery.

Base plate

Ideally, you need a large, flat surface to support the embroidery hoop. If possible, the machine should be set into a table. There are advantages to using a flat-bed machine, rather than a free arm with an extension, as you have a reasonably-sized surface which is smooth, while sometimes an extension will be angled, which causes problems by tilting the hoop. Some extensions make access to the bobbin difficult.

Weight of machine

Ideally, your machine should be light enough to be portable, but have sufficient weight to be stable. Some of the small compact machines cause problems with vibrations and instability.

If you are unsure of the location or operating of any of the features mentioned here, consult the manufacturer's instruction book.

The Old Cottage garden

left The painted background. Lines of resist have been used as guidelines within the foliage in the top half of the composition and kept to a minimum within the stonework

below, left All the dark tones in the foliage are embroidered in straight stitch in various directions to describe the different types of leaves. Two shades of dark brown are used to outline the steps and stone wall in straight stitch, allowing the dyed silk to represent the stones.

below, right The most distant trees and bushes are completed in straight stitches of various greens and yellows. Mid tones of green are worked in the foreground foliage. The white flowers are embroidered in a narrow width of zigzag. The flowers of the orange azalea are worked in running stitch in a circular motion

opposite The lightest shade of green is added to the foliage. Three shades of brown are used for the small bush on the right, darkest tone first. A light green is embroidered between the white flowers in a diagonal direction to represent the growth.

2
SOURCE
MATERIAL:
IDEAS AND
DESIGNS

5 Garden scene

Having adapted the machine for creative embroidery, the first stage is to design a picture. You will need source material, in the form of sketches or photographs. These are a means to an end – the embroidery is the creative process – but this is nonetheless an important and essential stage. The composition must be considered carefully; there is too much time and energy put into the embroidery to waste on an unsuitable or ill-conceived design.

If you are daunted by the thought of going out and gathering source material by sketching and drawing, perhaps the solution is photography. I was fortunate in enjoying a good art training which included a lot of observational drawing and painting, and I realise the importance of this as a good grounding in art and design. Having spent a lot of time translating three dimensions into two, I understand the drawing process well and for me the photograph I take serves as a good substitute for the landscape. When I embroider I am drawing or painting in stitch directly on to the fabric. I no longer use drawing to record my ideas and compositions; I use photography, with embroidery acting as the drawing stage.

Photography

Photography is an excellent way of recording the colour and detail references for embroideries. It can take minutes, rather than the hours needed for sketching or painting, which you may feel incapable of doing. If you feel unable to take your own photographs, magazines and books are a good source of images which you can copy or adapt. I prefer to go out and photograph my own compositions. The choice of scene is then mine, and I also experience a landscape or garden for myself, which I believe gives an extra dimension to my embroideries.

A simple autofocus camera is adequate: there are many makes to choose from. It is good enough to record composition ideas, colour and texture, giving sufficient in-formation to work from and a good starting point to an embroidery. They are, however, a little restrictive in that poor weather or lighting conditions can result in disappointing photographs.

I use a single-lens reflex (SLR) camera which has auto-exposure. It automatically sets the precise shutter speed for proper exposure at the set aperture, but even so allows considerable control over the results. For good pictures, where no specific effect is desired, the camera guides you to select the correct aperture and takes care of the shutter speed. This provides as much depth of field as possible while producing a shutter speed fast enough to stop the motion of most subjects.

Using a camera of this type also offers the creative flexibility to obtain certain effects, such as rendering a certain range or object in sharp focus to emphasise it against an out-of-focus background, or the ability to take good photographs in poor lighting conditions by altering the shutter speed accordingly. The camera also has the facility to fit wide-angle, telephoto and zoom lenses, giving great scope for close, detailed work and a variety of other types of shot. It is still only a means to an end, however, and for the embroiderer who merely seeks inspiration and the recording of ideas, a simple camera is all you need.

Looking at the view through the camera lens is the design stage of the picture. You are forced to isolate areas in the landscape rather than looking at the whole. This helps to develop an eye for good composition. It is a good idea to take lots of photographs of your subject matter, from different angles and heights – sitting or standing makes a difference to what you can see and will change dramatically the position of the horizon within the frame.

Take close-up photographs of tree bark, grass, flowers etc.; these will be useful when deciding the types of mark that make up certain textures in a landscape and therefore the types of stitch or technique that will be appropriate. Even if the detail is not included in the final embroidery, it will aid your understanding of objects around you and how they are constructed.

Having considered my subject matter and its subtle variations in colour, I have found that Fuji film is superior, due to its excellent analysis of shades of green.

Composition and design

Landscapes vary tremendously in terms of patterns and shapes found within them; for example, the mountains and hills of the Lake District to the flat patchwork fields of the Shropshire plain. Both offer interesting and diverse subject matter, with a different col-

6 Framing a composition with the camera

our scheme, range of textures and feel about them.

The paintings of well-known artists can be a great inspiration. They can provide ideas for compositions and ways of interpreting them in fabric and stitch. Analysing the style of painting and the features in a composition can help you understand which elements within a landscape you find appealing and which style you would like to emulate. Familiarise yourself with the following.

Joseph Mallard William Turner (1775–1851) was a great British painter with an intuitive understanding of nature. In his work the emphasis is on the effect of light within a landscape, the key elements being sunrises, mists and passing storms. He transformed everything into colour, of which he had a wonderful understanding, not in a decorative way but on an emotional level.

John Constable (1776–1837) was a painter of landscapes which are strong in design and composition. They breathe light, movement and atmosphere, achieved with scattered highlights and touches of pure colour.

Works of the **Impressionist** movement, i.e. painters such as **Claude Monet** (1840–1926), provide a wonderful selection of landscapes to study. They rejected the naturalist style of painting and instead aimed at capturing the impression of atmosphere, light and space. The way they painted changed our way of seeing colours within a landscape. Monet's particular interests were clouds, rain, sunshine, water and reflections.

The movement and rhythms found in the brushstrokes in the paintings of **Van Gogh** (1853–90) are a great inspiration for translation into stitches. Some of his landscapes are

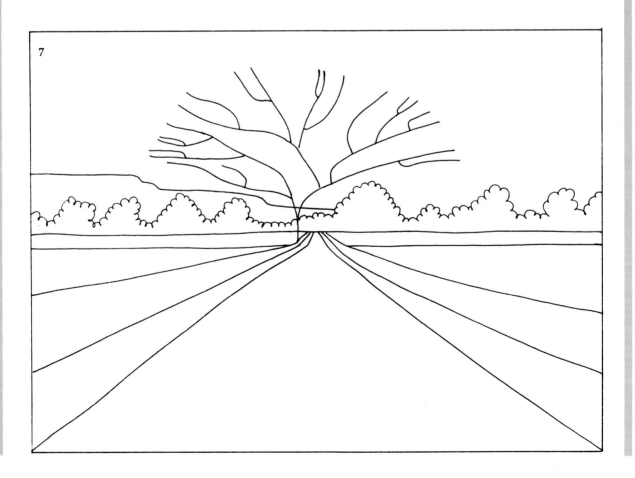

very simple in their composition; the emphasis is on heightened colours, simplication of form, and strong brush strokes which produce paintings of great power and presence.

Observe paintings by these artists and others; analyse what you like about them. What elements do they contain? Notice the proportion of sky to land, also the focal point and perspective.

When taking photographs or sketching, look for compositions in a landscape. You may, for example, be attracted to a certain tree because of its shape or colour. Consider where to place it in the frame. If it is to be the focal point, it should be off-centre. In figs 7 and 8 the tree is placed to the right of the picture, which results in the coverging lines of hedge and roadway not being symmetrical and is therefore more interesting.

Take several photographs with the tree in various positions within the frame and choose the best composition.

The position of the horizon makes a great difference to a design. A large proportion of sky gives a feeling of spaciousness while a high horizon, giving a larger proportion of land mass, will give greater distance. Either way, the horizon, like the focal point, should be off-centre. While sitting in a cornfield taking photographs you would have ears of corn above your head, breaking across the sky and the trees on the horizon. They make bold sweeping shapes, giving foreground interest, and a high horizon, giving distance to the design. Adding a large object in the foreground, such as details of flowers or trees, will help give a picture depth. If these do not occur naturally, two photographs could be combined to give the same effect.

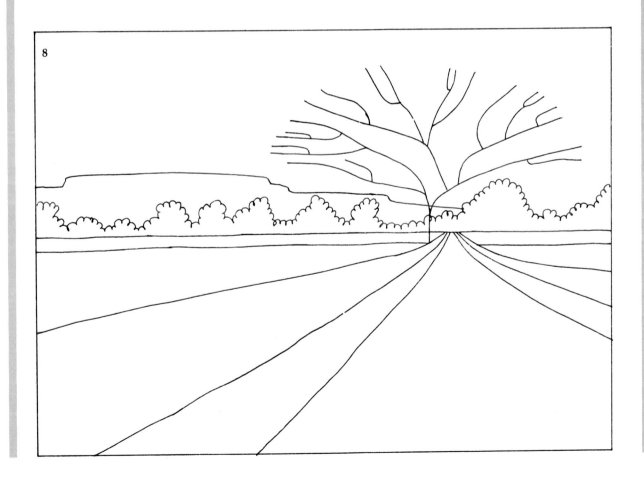

Poppies and cow parsley

above The painted background. The distant hills will not be embroidered, which will help give the composition depth

opposite, below The dark tones are worked in straight stitch

opposite, top Sage, olive and then light green worked on the trees in the middle distance in a small straight stitch. A mid tone of green is embroidered in the foreground. The cornfield on the left is embroidered with horizontal straight stitch in a matching colour to give a little texture rather than colour

overleaf With off-white in the bobbin and green on top, together with a tighter top tension, a straight stitch is used for the highlights on the bushes surrounding the poppy field. A salmon pink is embroidered in a horizontal straight stitch for the distant poppies, progressing to a horizontally-worked small zigzag. These increase in size towards the foreground and change to a deeper shade of red. The cow parsley is worked in a similar technique, using white thread. Finally a vertical straight stitch is worked with green thread in the foreground between the poppies and cow parsley

Poppies and cow parsley:
the finished embroidery

Notice the elements in a landscape which emphasise the distance, such as trees that diminish in size, their trunks getting progressively thinner as they get farther away, or dry-stone walls cutting across the composition, with individual stones clearly defined close to but becoming indistinct until the wall is eventually seen as a line stretching toward the horizon. The size of the fields they surround become smaller too.

You will be aware of more detail in objects close to, such as individual leaves on the branch of a tree cutting across the foreground of a picture, whereas trees in the distance are seen in terms of their overall shape. Flowers in the foreground are seen as individual shapes, but in the distance you are only aware of the shape they make growing together in a group in a herbaceous border or their distribution amongst the grasses in a field (figs 13 and 14).

An understanding of all this helps to develop a sense of depth and distance in a picture. Features which follow or form actual lines of perspective have a similar effect. The line of a fence, ploughed field, path or road disappearing over a hill leads your eye into the picture, maybe drawing your attention toward the focal point of a group of trees or a stone bridge (fig 15).

The composition also needs structure, something to link together the individual elements, such as a meandering river or road or an interesting-shaped branch cutting across the design with bits of the landscape appearing above and below. Added to this should be balance, created by one feature balancing another within the frame, for example a group of poppies in the foreground balanced by a row of trees on the horizon. There should be a balance between areas of interest, some busy with detail,

10 This photograph was combined with Fig 11 (below) for the composition of the embroidery in Fig 12 (overleaf)

others quiet, peaceful, somewhere to rest the eye – such as a smooth lawn, or an expanse of clear sky, combined with areas of activity that are full of interest, colour and detail, such as a flower border in summer or a field full of poppies, daisies and corn. These make positive and negative areas, both of which are needed in a composition.

Designs need a focal point, and will be more successful if this is placed one-third in from the left or right, top or bottom of the frame. It should not be placed in the centre. The focal point need not be a feature, such as a tree or group of buildings, but could be an area of activity, contrast or interest arising from colour or texture. It is somewhere to which the eye is first drawn before it takes in the rest of the picture.

Another element to consider in a picture is atmosphere, created by the subject matter, for example the intimacy of a heavily

wooded area, with the feeling of the trees close around you; the curiosity aroused by glimpses of a garden through an archway creating an atmosphere of secrecy; sunlight and shadows dappling a carpet of autumn leaves; or a garden path curving out of sight, inviting you to walk along it. Try to create a magical quality to a picture, something to fire people's imagination.

If you are working from photographs from magazines or books and are not entirely happy with the composition, try cutting a window in a piece of card or paper. Cut it the same proportions that you want your embroidery to be. Move the window over the photograph to frame several different areas. When you find a section with the elements you require, tape the window in position. This area can be enlarged. Take a simple tracing of the section of the photograph – the outline of shapes, not any

16

17 Focal point or point of
interest, to be placed on
any of these lines or where
they meet, such as the
tree in Fig 15

18

Summer shadows

above All the dark tones are embroidered within the distant trees and the tree in the foreground. A mid tone of green is added to the distant trees with straight stitch. The lines of cut grass are embroidered in the small field on the right. With these details completed, features which cut across them can now be worked. The foliage of the foreground tree is embroidered with a small whip stitch with a dark green and a mid green thread

opposite, top Olive green and rust are embroidered on the hedge, in the middle distance, in a small straight stitch. Horizontal straight stitches are used for the stripes of cut grass, towards the foreground these become horizontal bands of short vertical straight stitches. The cow parsley is embroidered in a narrow width of zigzag worked on the spot. A mid green is embroidered on the tree in the foreground

opposite, below Detail of the composition

overleaf Using a small whip stitch with dark green in the bobbin and a light green or yellow on top, the final highlights are added to the foliage of the tree. Cream and beige horizontal straight stitches are worked between the stripes of cut grass. Light green vertical straight stitches are worked between the cow parsley. A lighter shade of rust is added to the hedge

Summer shadows:
the finished embroidery

details. Divide this into small squares, like a grid. Draw a square or rectangle the size you want your embroidery to be on a piece of paper. Divide this into the same number of squares as the tracing. Transfer the lines from the squares on the tracing paper to the corresponding squares on the paper until the entire design is complete. This method can be used to enlarge, reduce, or change the proportions of the tracing or of a whole photograph. Whatever size the tracing or the final design, they must be divided into the same number of squares for this technique to work.

If you do not wish to change the basic composition in terms of size or proportion, you may want to move or eliminate certain elements; for example if there are too many trees on the horizon, thin them out or remove sections to make a more interesting distribution. Telegraph poles or electricity pylons may spoil a scene, so simply remove them. Perhaps the photograph has a stormy or dramatic cloud formation which you find too distracting or too difficult to paint; simplify it to a wash of pale blue or use the sky from another photograph. Don't be afraid to

19 Framing an area of the picture

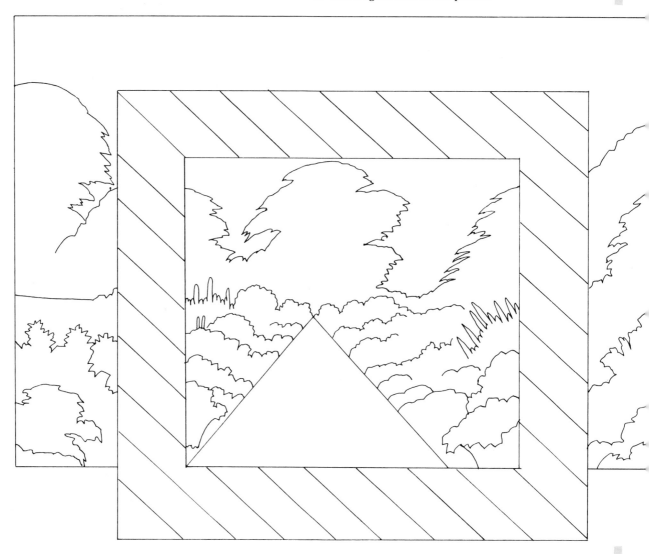

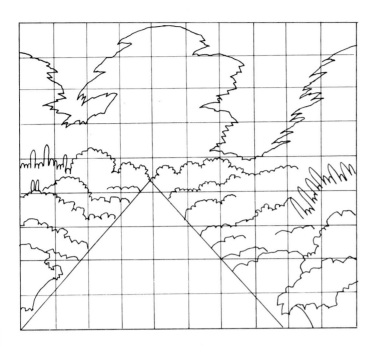

20 A tracing of the framed composition divided into a grid

remove elements which you may have difficulty in embroidering, and if necessary replace them with details you can work.

Tone and colour

Tone is not the same as colour. To think in terms of tone you must think in terms of black and white photography, where all the colours are transformed into shades of grey. One colour can be many different tones; pale green will be a lighter tone than dark green, but they are the same colour. Two different colours can have the same tonal value. You need to analyse the tonal values in a composition because lack of tonal variation in a picture causes it to look flat.

Contrast in tone and colour in the foreground gives an area density. The variations in tone are strongest there and then become softer into the distance. In the foreground you should find bright greens and yellows in grass, vibrant reds and blues for poppies and cornflowers; dashes of white daisies will brighten the area even more, or rich shades of russet, brown and yellow in an autumn hedgerow. As fields or flowers diminish in scale towards the horizon they not only become paler in tone but also the colours change. Trees become pale blue-green, grey or beige, mountains become shades of purple and grey, and poppies change to a pale orange or peach. Colours become colder in the distance. Try seeing a composition in terms of light and dark areas; these require balancing with each other.

Different areas in a picture can be linked by the use of colour. A pale pink-beige ploughed field on the horizon will be picked up to good effect in the deeper shades of that colour used for flowers or dry grasses elsewhere in the picture. Varying proportions of each colour, especially complementary colours such as red and green, yellow and purple, or orange and blue, can create interesting effects. For example, small touches of red against large areas of green actually make you more aware of the green. Colour creates atmosphere. The obvious examples are blues, greys and purples, which are cold and wintery. Rusts, browns and golds imply autumn; yellow, acid or lime greens and white give the fresh vitality associated with spring. Bright primary colours – reds, yellows and blues – mixed with green give summer brightness.

You may wish to analyse and then change the colour in the photograph you are using as a reference for an embroidery. By changing the intensity of the colours, different effects can be created. I heightened the foreground colours in *Cut hayfield* to improve the balance and the depth. I embroidered the shades of rust, sand and beige in the cut stubble of the field, and made the greens in

21 The composition lines transferred to a larger-scale grid of different proportions

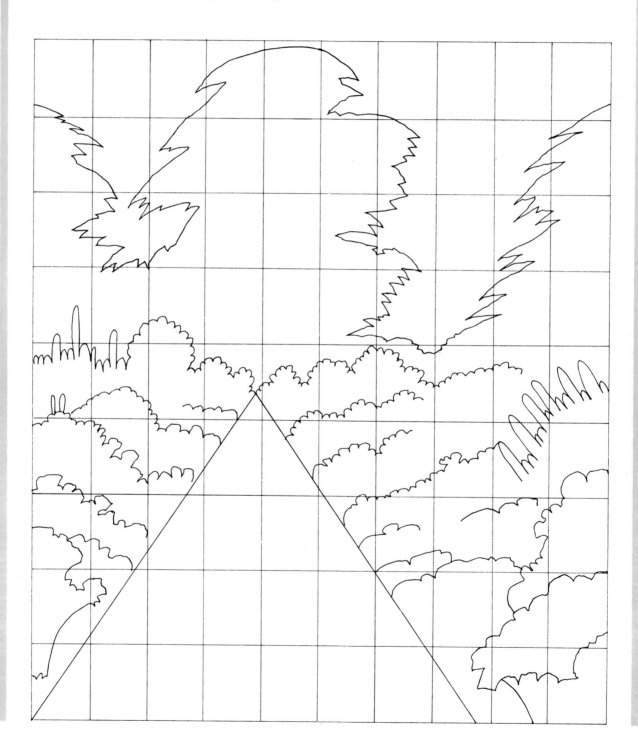

22 Areas of contrast in the foreground and cooler colours in the distance

the hay much stronger in the foreground. It served to add distance to the picture and emphasised the pattern element in the stripes of hay, giving them a richness which I remember from being there but that the camera had not recorded.

You can change the whole feel and atmosphere of a photograph. An early spring landscape can become a riot of summer colour, as richer, bluer greens for grass and trees and a blue sky make all the colours warmer and more vibrant. A daytime photograph of a winter tree silhouetted against a cold grey sky can be changed into a dramatic evening sunset, rich and warm with reds, yellows and oranges. Experiment with different ideas and colour schemes – one photograph could potentially supply the inspiration for several embroideries.

23 *Roadside poppies*

24 *Cut hayfield*

Brogyntyn Park

above Small running stitches are worked in a circular motion for the dark tones in the distant foliage. Vertical lines of running stitch are used to describe the shape of the two tree trunks, using four shades of brown. These are smooth-barked trees, which could have been left just painted, but I felt that they needed the emphasis of stitch. Dark brown is used in a horizontal running stitch in a spiralling motion for the carpet of leaves.

opposite, top A small whip stitch, with yellow and white thread, is used in the distance. Mid greens and yellow-greens are added using the same technique. A lighter shade of brown is worked amongst the previous stitches for the fallen leaves

opposite, below Dark and mid green running stitches are worked for the bluebell stems and leaves in the foreground. Two more shades of brown are added to the fallen leaves using the same technique. The first few leaves hanging down in the middle distance are drawn in zigzag. The bluebells are embroidered in a narrow zigzag

overleaf Light green running stitches are used to highlight the bluebell stems and leaves. Finally, the large leaves cutting across the front of the composition are drawn in with a zigzag. It was important in this picture to use very small stitches in the distance to emphasise the larger-scale stitches in the foreground. Without any obvious lines of perspective, it is this that creates the sense of depth

Brogyntyn Park:
the finished embroidery

3
FABRICS AND COLOUR

We have now gathered inspiration, and information in the form of photographs, sketches or both, then considered the elements that make up a composition and explored them in terms of tone and colour. The next stage is to decide on a fabric and apply colour to it as a base for embroidery.

Each type and weight of fabric has different properties; they absorb dyes at varying rates, therefore several different fabrics immersed in a dye bath for the same length of time would come out in various shades; also the same quantity of dye on a brush will spread a lot further on fine, thin silk than on a heavy weight calico. The skill is to experiment, take notes and discover how each fabric behaves and turn the information to your advantage.

There are many ways of changing the colour of the fabric you choose to embroider on. The subject matter, scale of working, and type of embroidery in mind will suggest the fabric and way to apply the colour. As a general rule, the bolder the embroidery techniques, the heavier the weight of fabric you should use. All ways of applying colour can be used on any fabric: some are more successful or effective on one fabric than on another. I would suggest that you experiment with all the methods discussed on a cheaper alternative fabric of a similar weight; for example the results will be similar on a heavyweight calico to on raw silk.

Before dying your fabric it should be washed to remove any dressing the manufacturer may have used, which may repel the dye. When dry, stretch it on to a wooden frame. This provides a flat surface of material which will take the dye evenly. It should be stretched over the front of the frame to keep the fabric away from the table. The piece of material must be a few inches larger than the frame to enable you to hold the fabric to stretch it taut. I use a simple wooden frame made out of lengths of 1 in × 1 in (2.5 cm × 2.5 cm) pine. The frame is 16 in × 16 in (40 cm × 40 cm), large enough to stretch ¼ in (0.25 m) of fabric on, and to paint

one large or two smaller backgrounds. Leave approximately 4 in (10 cm) around a design so that there is enough material to grip when stretching it in the embroidery hoop. I use silk pins, which have three small points rather than one long one like a traditional drawing pin. These hold the fabric taut with less likelihood of tearing.

When stretching the fabric, try not to distort the weave, and keep the weft threads at right angles to the warp. With the frame on a table, place the fabric over it.

1 Pin along one edge of the frame, starting at the centre point and pulling the fabric taut, 2–3 in (5–7.5 cm) place the pins evenly apart.
2 Stretch the fabric to the opposite side, keeping the weave parallel to the frame.
3 Start in the centre again and, pulling the fabric, line up the pins with the first row.
4 Stretch up the two remaining sides in the same manner to achieve an even tension.

Gather your equipment (dyes, brushes and water pot) around you. Protect the table and yourself with newspaper and apron respectively. For practice, you can use watercolour or acrylic paints, coloured inks, felt pens, crayons – anything that will provide colour. These are all fine to experiment with, but you must use the appropriate dye or fabric paint on the fabric you intend to embroider on. You will want the colour to be permanent, lightfast and, in some cases, washable (if you are embroidering clothes or cushions, for example). All dyes and paints will state in the manufacturer's instructions which fabrics they are suitable for and how to 'fix' the dye to the fabric.

I would suggest that the first background you paint is small enough to fit completely in the embroidery hoop. This will allow you to embroider without having to restretch your work, and it is easier to work on a composite hoop. It is rather wasteful to paint one small design in the centre of ¼ in (0.25 m) of fabric, so either paint three or four, or just

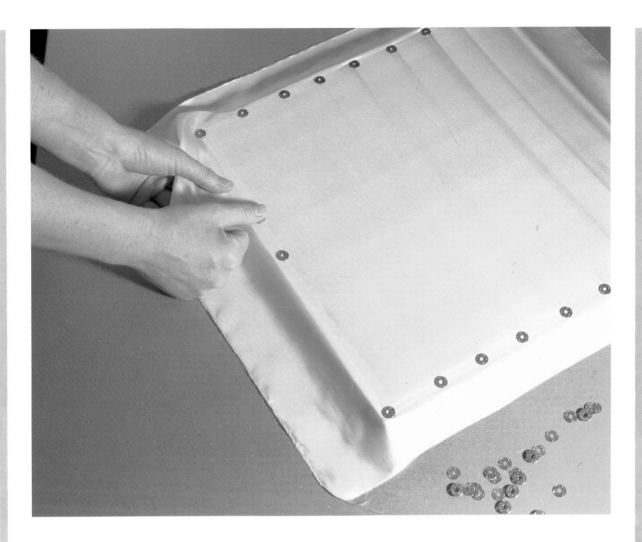

26 Stretching silk on a wooden frame

stretch in the embroidery hoop enough fabric to paint it on. It can be a good idea to paint two identical backgrounds, one to experiment on and the other to complete when you have discovered the effect you want.

I use Habutai silk for my embroideries. My preference for silk for painting and embroidering goes back to college days when experimenting with dying fabrics, and being so pleased with the results on silk. It has quality, and its subtle sheen compliments beautifully the texture of stitch in my embroideries. Also, for areas which I do not embroider, for reasons of compositional balance, there is no better fabric for my work.

Its fine weave and smooth appearance are well suited to the scale of detail in my work.

I use dyes in preference to fabric paints, as they retain the characteristic sheen of the silk because they are absorbed by the fabric, unlike paint which can sit on the surface. The Habutai silk does not absorb a lot of dye due to its light weight. The dye spreads rapidly across the surface and so can be difficult to control, as is preventing one colour running into another. A certain amount of control is achieved if the fabric is dry and you use a small brush with very little dye on it; this is also useful for painting in details. The solution to controlling the dye on this weight of fabric is to use a resist or outliner.

27 Silk pins and the equipment for painting on silk

A woodland stream

left After deciding the stream would look more natural painted than embroidered, great care was taken with this area, working with small brushes and letting each colour dry before applying the next.

below, left The foliage in the distance is worked in a spiralling running stitch following the diagonal direction of the branches. Various tree trunks are embroidered in a closely-worked zigzag. A dark brown is used to emphasise the edge of the stream, a running stitch following the contour of the bank and worked horizontally at the water's edge

below, right Flecks of yellow are embroidered into the distant foliage. The mid and lighter tones are then added to create depth. The stitches are small and all follow the same direction. Broad leaf shapes are drawn in zigzag in the foreground

opposite The middle distance tree trunks are completed. Lighter tones are embroidered within the foliage. The foreground trunks and branches are embroiderd in zigzag. The tree trunk on the left is embroidered finally using four shades of brown. The ridges in the bark are embroidered in a narrow width of zigzag worked vertically with running stitches in between. A third shade of green is added to the foreground leaves worked in zigzag. The bluebells are embroidered with small rows of zigzag. Finally, larger leaves in the trees embroidered in a wide zigzag in yellow and light green add to the depth

Resist

This is a clear, gel-like substance which, when applied to fabric, forms a barrier between two colours. It is used to outline the design, to separate one colour from another and to retain the colour of the fabric if required. It must be applied to dry fabric and allowed to dry before the dye is painted on. It is applied in a plastic pipette with a metal nib. The nibs are available in various sizes. If they are too fine, they clog up easily with the resist as you work. I use a No. 6 nib, which gives a thick enough line to form a barrier but is not too thick to interfere with the composition. There is a wire supplied with the nib; when not in use, leave this in the nib

to prevent the resist drying up and blocking it. Take care to draw a continuous line, as any breaks or weaknesses and the dye will break through.

Hold the pipette upside down at the same angle as you would hold a pen. Apply a gentle pressure to squeeze out the resist and draw slowly and smoothly with the nib as if it were a pencil. Practise drawing on the stretched fabric; you need to co-ordinate the pressure on the pipette with the speed you draw, to get a smooth line of consistent width.

Work with the photograph and design sketch in view. With the resist, draw a

28 Drawing out the composition with resist

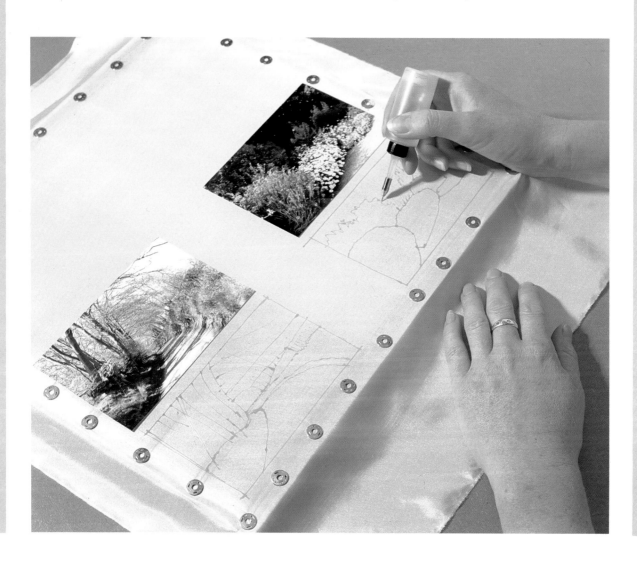

square the size the final composition is to be. Outline the sections of the design in terms of blocks of colour. When drawing with the resist, it can help to think of it as a white pen, because that is the end result when you have applied the dye. Wherever you draw with it remains the colour of the silk. The white lines between the blocks of colour are easily covered with embroidery. Keep this stage as simple as possible: a minimum of white lines will give you greater flexibility at the embroidery stage. For example, simply outline the shape of a wall – do not draw in every brick or stone in resist, which can be done later with stitch, giving a finer line than it would take to cover the white line left by the resist.

If an area is to be covered with embroidery, you may want to put in some guidelines in resist for the position of flowers in a bed, for example, knowing that the white lines will easily be covered. Resist can be used effectively for shading areas in white (the colour of the silk), such as clouds. I have produced a great number of skies using the resist in a cross-hatching type of shading. When painted over, some of the dye penetrates the resist to the fabric and produces a soft blurred effect, ideal for the edges of clouds. Resist is used for outlining, drawing or shading and for putting in guidelines for shapes that will be covered in embroidery.

Painting on resist with a brush will give quite different effects. Use a stiff brush to streak resist across a sky or area of water; paint a wash of colour over it and the resist creates subtle white lines. Some features should be outlined smaller than required, trees for example. Where sky or background colour shows through the outer edges of a tree, this area should be left to be embroidered. Think in terms of background colour: do not use the resist to draw small details and features that should be embroidered.

When the outliner is dry and you have checked that all the lines are continuous, you are ready to paint on the dyes.

Mixing and painting with dyes

I use the water-based Deka silk dyes, for several reasons: they are available in a good range of strong colours, they are easy to 'fix' to the fabric, they can be used on cotton, silk or synthetic fabrics, they are highly fade-resistant, even when diluted, and they come in a liquid form which is easy to paint with. All colours are intermixable and just need water to lighten them in shade.

When the resist is dry and the background is ready to paint, mix all the colours you are going to need. Use a white palette designed for mixing water-colour paints. The white will enable you to see the colours you are mixing. Always test a little colour on the fabric, remembering that it will dry a shade lighter. Mix enough dye for each area to be painted. Match the colours in the photograph as closely as possible. Understanding how to mix colours to achieve a certain shade can be daunting. There are a few simple rules which may help.

There are three primary colours – red, yellow and blue – from which, in theory, all other colours can be made. Experimenting with mixing dyes will teach you a lot, but understanding the basic rules will help.

Equal amounts of

Red and yellow *make* orange

red and blue *make* purple

blue and yellow *make* green

} these are secondary colours

You can go on to mix these colours together to make many more, such as ochre, sienna, violet, crimson, grey and black. It can be a lot simpler and quicker to buy a larger range of dyes than just the primary colours, to cut out a lot of the mixing stages.

Deka silk dyes are available in eighteen different colours, but for ease of mixing I would start with a range of the following: primary yellow, red, blue, dark green, sienna, ochre and black.

Knowing the three primary colours, and which two combine to make the secondary colours, will help when trying to mix the colour you want. If a green dye is too blue in shade, it needs yellow adding; if it is too yellow it needs blue, and so on. If a colour is too dark in shade, add more water; this is the same as adding white. If a colour is too bright, try adding small amounts of grey or brown to tone it down. With practice and experimenting, you will be able to mix the colours you need.

Use a range of brush sizes. I use water-colour brushes on the Habutai silk, in sizes No. 0, No. 2 and No. 5. The smaller the area to paint, the smaller the brush to use. You need to judge how much dye is necessary to fill an area: too much, and it will flood over the line of resist. Fill a brush with dye and, on a practice piece, make one brushstroke and see how far the dye will spread on its own. Do this with several sizes of brush and it will give you an idea of which size to use for a certain area.

When painting within an outline, keep the brush strokes ¼ in (0.5 cm) from the line of resist and let the dye spread up to it. When cleaning your brush to go from one colour to another in the palette, squeeze out the excess clean water with your fingers: this will stop you making the colour paler.

You do not need to paint in details if you intend to cover an area in stitches, in which case a simple wash of colour will suffice. A field may have several shades of green in it, which will be put in embroidery. The background colour should be one shade of green that will show between the stitches. If the overall effect is of an area shading from light to dark, this could also be applied to the painting. In some cases, the dyed silk is a more integral part of the embroidery: for example, a wall or pathway that will be interpreted with running stitch outlining

29 Test the colours before applying them to the composition, remembering they will dry lighter in tone

bricks, stones or pebbles with the silk showing between. The greatest care needs to be taken when painting an area where there is to be no embroidery to cover any mistakes! I always paint these areas first, then if a disaster occurs I don't waste time painting the rest. It is a shame to paint a composition background to perfection and then make a mistake on the sky which cannot be disguised with stitches.

As a general rule, paint the sky paler rather than darker; it is better to be subtle in this area. Unless it is a dramatic sunset, and the focal point of the picture, then you should enjoy yourself and be bold.

Paint in some details rather than embroidering them; this could be where you want detail but not the texture that stitch provides. In this case it is even more important to use the right size of brush and not to overload it with dye. More control can be achieved if each colour dries before the next is applied. For example, if painting reflections in water, paint a background wash and let it dry. Then, using a small brush, paint in the reflections of the tree or fence over the first colour. If you want colours to merge or blur at the edges, have them both wet at the same time. For greater control, use small amounts of dye on dry fabric.

An interesting effect can be obtained by painting an area and, before it dries, dabbing a small wet brush, but not one full of water, all over it. The areas where you dab will go a little paler and create a mottled appearance, suggesting a pebbled or gravel pathway, perhaps. This can also be done with a small brush dipped in a dye of another colour.

When the background painting is complete, let it dry thoroughly. To fix the dye to the fabric you must iron on the reverse side for two or three minutes with the iron on silk setting, with a piece of waste material to protect the ironing-board cover. This will make the fabric washable up to 60°C, dry-cleanable and lightfast.

To remove the resist, wash in a mixture of liquid soap or soap flakes and hot water.

Rinse thoroughly. This is now ready to iron whilst still damp, to avoid creases drying in the silk.

Painting without resist

You can paint successfully on dye without using resist. It is better to use medium to heavy-weight material, such as calico or raw silk (silk noile), which is dense enough to absorb the dye so that it does not spread too far. Resist would not easily penetrate this thickness of fabric sufficiently to form a barrier, but because it has similar properties to painting canvas, you can paint on it in a similar way. You should use a stiff brush, the type used for oil or acrylic paints, and not overload it with dye.

A sharp outline is easy to obtain if you do this. If you require the dye to run, to blend one colour with another or to blur or soften an edge, for a misty horizon, for example, wet the fabric in that area with clean water and paint over it. The properties of the fabric change when it is wet; it becomes easier for the dye to spread into the wet area. With practice, you will have good control on this type of fabric by keeping areas dry and wetting others to achieve the effect you want.

Spraying

Another way to apply colour is to spray the dye or paint on to the fabric. This can be a messy process, so protect yourself and your work area from overspray. Try a simple diffuser which you blow through or, for larger, more ambitious projects, an airbrush. Spraying works well in conjunction with stencils – shapes cut out of card to mask certain areas whilst spraying others. This will result in a hard-edged outline against the stencil and a soft, blurred edge where you have sprayed away from it. You can spray one colour on top of another to blend

30 The reflections in the stream are painted

31 A silk noile painted
and embroidered
cushion

32 A tracing of the composition to be cut up as
    pattern pieces

33 The fabric with 1.5 cm (½ in) allowance at the
    sides and base of the shape

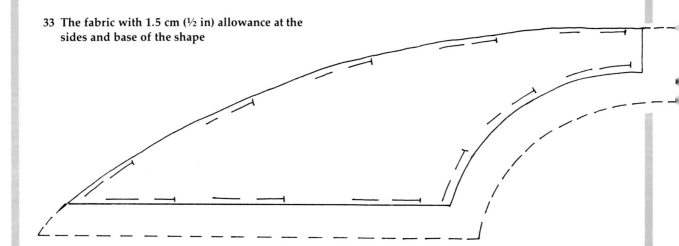

them, or overlap the edges to shade from one colour to another. The paint or dye needs to be thin enough to spray through the diffuser, but not too watery, otherwise it will spread underneath the edge of the stencil. This technique will work well on most weights of fabric; let each colour you spray dry before you go on to the next, otherwise it will run.

This is a very interesting technique, as the stencils give control of the shape you spray and the combination of hard-edged outlines and misty areas is very effective.

Stippling

You can also dab on the paint or dye using stencils, but they need to be slightly thicker for this. You can stipple on the dye with a stiff brush or dab it on with a piece of sponge, cotton-wool balls, screwed-up paper or rags dipped into a tray of dye and patted over the fabric. They will all give different textures and soft edges. Again, different results will be achieved if working on wet rather than dry fabric. If too much dye is applied at once, the texture each object gives will be blurred and lost.

These techniques of dabbing or spraying will give broad areas of colour, and if you allow them to dry first, details can be painted on with a small brush. Try a simple composition divided into one-third sky and two-thirds land. Wet the fabric at the top only, and with a large brush paint a wash of different blues for the sky, merging them together. Let this dry and stipple the rest in greens to represent fields. When this is dry, using a small brush, details can be added, such as trees and a fence on the horizon, as can details you do not wish to embroider, like the lines of a ploughed field in the distance.

Dye bath

Another way to colour the background is to dye a range of fabrics and colours in a dye bath, then cut them into pieces to form a collage.

Cold water dyes are the easiest to use and will successfully dye natural fibres such as cotton and silk. Mix them according to the manufacturer's instructions in a plastic bucket or bowl. The fabric must be stirred or agitated continuously whilst in the dye bath to ensure that it dyes evenly. For patterned or textured results, try tying or twisting the material before it is immersed in the bath.

Variations in colour can be achieved by placing different weights and types of fabric in the same bath for the same length of time, as they all absorb the dye differently and will all vary in shade. The dye will reach its full strength in the time stated by the manufacturer, but you can leave it in for less time to achieve paler tones. Fabric can also be placed in two different colours, one after another: for example, in a green bath until full strength, then a yellow bath for five minutes to give an olive green result.

Blue and green may be the only two baths needed to dye fabric for a landscape composition, but with the addition of, for example, yellow or brown, many more colours can be achieved by mixing. Refer to the section on painting with dyes – colour theory applies here, too.

To shade a colour from dark to light on one piece of fabric, you can dip-dye it. Leave all the material in the bath for five minutes, then slowly lift it out, leaving less and less in the bath to dye to full strength. This effect could be used in blue for a sky.

When you have dyed sufficient colours and shades to choose from, dry and fix the dye to the fabric by following the manufacturer's instructions.

Collage

To make a collage, take a tracing of the picture you are working from; as with painting the background, you are dividing the composition into simple blocks of colour.

The poppy garden

above The painted background for *The poppy garden*

opposite, top Two shades of dark green are embroidered for the trees and hedge in a closely worked running stitch. The same colours are used in running stitch for the dark tones amongst the foliage in the flower border

opposite, below A lighter shade of green is added to the trees, hedge and foliage. It provides the final highlight in the distance, but more shades will be necessary within the border. The pathway is embroi-

dered with three shades of brown in running stitches. The patch of soil is embroidered in running stitch, closely worked a horizontal direction. The flowers in the distance are embroidered in a narrow zigzag, worked on the spot

overleaf The foliage between the flowerheads is embroidered in running stitch. The poppies in the foreground are embroidered in a running stitch using four shades of red and pink. The poppy buds are embroidered in light green in a zigzag. The purple flowers in the foreground are worked in zigzag

The poppy garden:
the finished embroidery

Now cut up the tracing paper into these sections and use them as pattern pieces Pin each one to the appropriate piece of dyed fabric and cut it out, leaving 1.5 cm (½ in) allowance of fabric at the bottom and sides of each shape.

You will need a lightweight fabric such as muslin, as a backing fabric for this collage; it should be approximately 15 cm (6 in) larger than the design. This will give you material around the edge to stretch in the hoop when you are embroidering. Place all the pieces of dyed fabric in the centre of the muslin. Start with the top of the design and work down to the bottom, overlapping each piece by its 1.5 cm (½ in) allowance. Pin and tack these into position. If the shapes overlap, the advantage is that there is only one raw edge to sew down; also, when you stretch the collage in a hoop to embroider, the pieces will not come apart to reveal the backing fabric.

You are now ready to embroider on this the same way as if it were a painted background. In many designs, especially landscapes, features in the composition are often to be placed where two colours, i.e. fabrics, join, so use embroidery to sew down the raw edges – for example, where two fields meet you can embroider a hedge to join them. If this is not appropriate, use a matching thread to anchor down the fabric.

The type of stitch used is determined by what that area of the picture represents. If you do not want to be aware of the stitches joining the fabric, the scale of stitch used will help: for example a wide zigzag on a distant horizon would destroy depth achieved by use of colour and composition, while a small horizontal running stitch in a matching colour would be less obtrusive.

When working in collage, the fabrics you use or dye should not be too heavy. The combination of overlapped edges and the backing fabric could result in areas that are too thick to embroider on with ease.

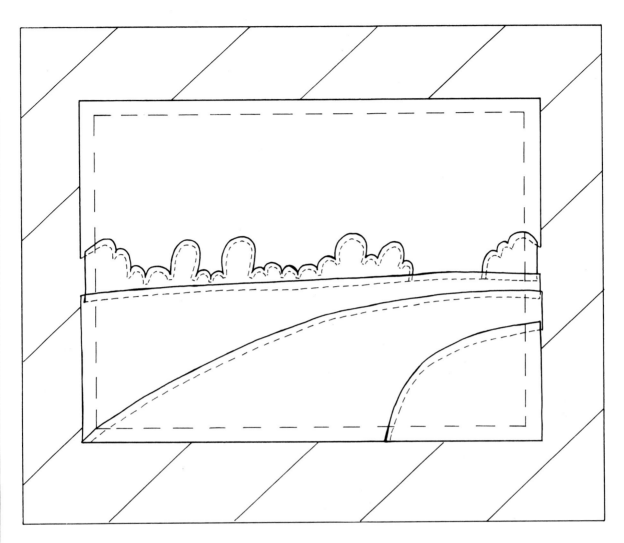

**34 All the overlapping collage pieces laid on the
backing muslin**

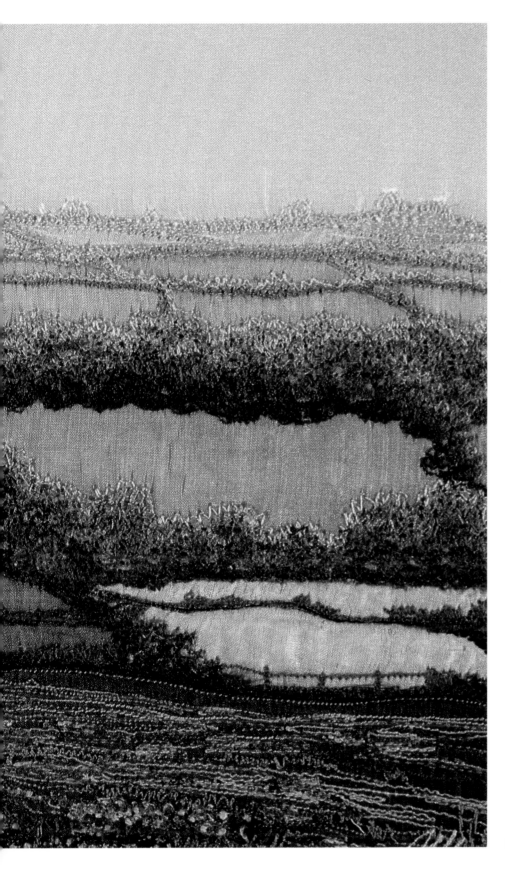

35 A dyed silk collage

Summer scene

above Quite a lot of detail has been painted in for this composition. The grass in the foreground will not be embroidered and the detail in the trees is not absolutely necessary but helps to create the depth and three-dimensional effect at an early stage

opposite, top The dark tones are embroidered in small running stitches following the direction of growth. Much more of this colour is applied than may appear necessary at first analysis, but it is essential to create the depth required

opposite, below The pink rhododendrons and the yellow azalea flowers are embroidered in a narrow zigzag. A lighter shade of green is added to the trees, providing the flecks of green which will show between the final yellow highlights

overleaf The yellow is embroidered on the trees to complete the three-dimensional effect

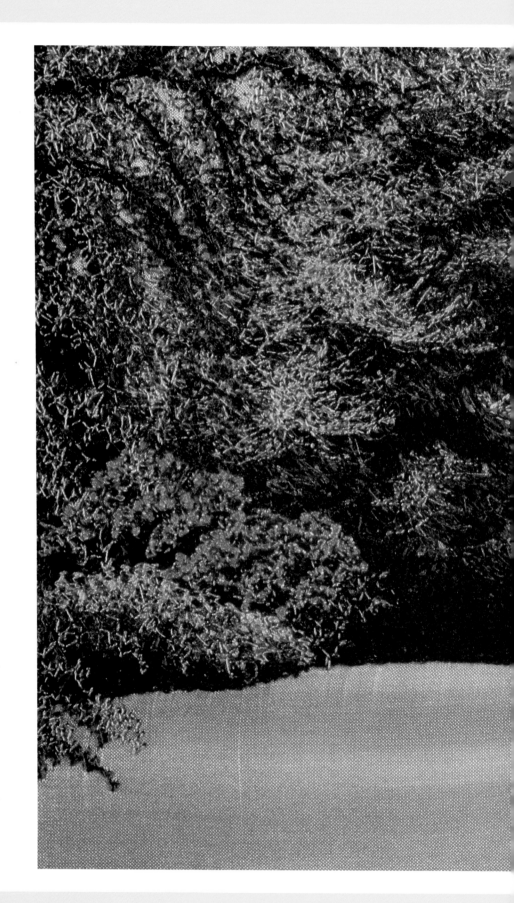

Summer scene:
the finished embroidery

4
EQUIPMENT FOR EMBROIDERY

36 Garden archway

Embroidery hoop

When the presser foot is removed it is necessary to stretch the fabric in an embroidery hoop to keep it flat on the bed of the machine. The hoop also supplies you with something to hold, helping to guide the fabric under the needle. The material must be as taut as a drum. It is essential that you take the time to achieve this, as it prevents the stitches gathering or puckering the fabric. It also avoids the fabric bouncing up and down within the hoop as the needle goes through it, which not only can cause the machine to miss stitches but also the thread to fray and then break.

I use a 20 cm (8 in) wooden embroidery hoop with the inner ring bound neatly with cotton tape or strips of fabric. This gives a better grip on the material you are stretching and prevents it becoming marked. This is important if your design is bigger than the hoop, because you will need to restretch the fabric to work on different areas of the design.

If the hoop is larger than 20 cm (8 in) it can be harder to stretch it really taut. You may also find that the space between the needle and the neck of the machine is so narrow that you have to turn your work sideways to work on some areas of the design, so that in some cases there could be an area in the centre of a larger hoop that you could not get under the needle. If the hoop is smaller than 20 cm (8 in), it will be necessary to move it several times to complete a small embroidery.

Make sure the hoop is shallow enough to fit under the needle in its highest position. Purchase one with a slot in the screw on the outer hoop to enable you to tighten it with a screwdriver, as you will not be able to tighten it sufficiently with your fingers. The fabric you are stretching in the hoop must be larger than it by approximately 10 cm (4 in) to enable you to grip the fabric to pull it taut. The best method to stretch the fabric is as follows:

1 Tighten the screw on the outer hoop until the inner hoop just fits inside it.
2 Place the outer hoop on a table.
3 Lay the fabric right side up over this hoop.
4 Push the inner hoop into position.
5 Tighten the screw a little.
6 With the hoop on the table, use thumbs and forefingers to grip the fabric outside of the hoop, and use remaining fingers to hold the hoops flat and prevent the inner hoop popping out of position.
7 Pull the fabric tight. Keep moving the hoop around and pulling, take care not to distort the weave of the fabric.
8 Tighten the screw and pull the fabric again.
9 Keep doing this until the screw will not tighten any more and the fabric is as tight as a drum.

I find this easier to do standing up, as I seem to have more leverage to pull the material through between the rings. Push the inner ring fractionally lower than the outer ring to ensure the fabric is touching the bed of the machine.

You may need to retighten the fabric in the hoop at various stages whilst embroidering, because working on it can cause it to loosen. When moving the hoop and restretching the fabric to embroider on another area of the design, take care to pull only on the areas of fabric without embroidery. Due to the texture of stitch it grips the bound inner hoop and will not pull through the hoops easily.

Threads

I use machine embroidery threads, such as Madeira Tanne No. 50, which are 100 per cent cotton and have an attractive sheen which compliments the silk fabric. They are available in an extensive range of colours. I also use polyester and cotton mixture threads of a similar thickness, which work in well with the tanne.

When beginning embroidery, I would recommend using a thicker thread, such as a

No. 40 or No. 50 or polyester or polyester and cotton mixture, which is stronger and therefore less likely to break than a fine, pure cotton thread. It is best to experiment with various threads to see which suits you and your machine best. You do not want the added frustration of breaking threads when trying to master machine embroidery.

Rayon threads have a distinctive shine, which is very attractive, but they can break quite easily and I feel they are unsuitable for the natural scenes and landscapes I produce. I think the subject matter should be considered when choosing threads.

Embroidery scissors

These need to be small, sharp and pointed to enable you to cut threads close to your work.

Needles

I use size 80 (12) needles, which are fine enough for silk but do not break too easily. In free embroidery, extra strain is put on the needle and thread due to the length of stitch being determined by you and not by the machine. The take-up lever pulls thread off the reel at the rate the fabric is moving in conventional sewing with the presser foot on. This does not apply in free embroidery, so that when the hoop is moved quickly under the needle strain is put on both the thread and the needle. The size of the needle should suit the weight of fabric you are working on – a 70 or 80 for fine silks, and up to 90 or 100 for heavyweight calico or silk.

Fabric

A medium to lightweight fabric is ideal to experiment on. Variations in the weight of fabric used could determine the scale of work, for example the finest silk suggests embroidery in a delicate detailed manner with small stitches in a fine thread, whilst the other extreme could be a fabric with slubs and texture in the weave, suggesting the couching of threads, bold lines of zigzag and stranded cotton used in the bobbin for moss stitch.

A whole composition could be made of a collage of different weights and types of fabric in the same colour, such as a fine silk on the horizon with the fabrics increasing in weight and texture towards the foreground. This could be dipped into a dye bath with interesting results.

Autumn parkland

left The background is a mixture of resist as guidelines for branches cutting across the sky and to mark the edges of the tree shapes. The grass has some detail painted into it because the intention is not to embroider it

below, left The branches cutting across the sky are worked in zigzag and the dark tones are embroidered in running stitch

below, right Two shades of green are added to the distant trees

opposite Two shades of yellow are embroidered in running stitch to highlight the trees. Finally, the foreground tree is completed. Four shades of brown and rust are selected. Starting with the darkest tone, leaf shapes are drawn in zigzag; they all face different directions. This is continued with the other three shades, building up depth and the shape of the branches

5
EMBROIDERY TEXTURES AND TECHNIQUES

37 Detail of The Poppy Garden

Preparing the machine for free embroidery

If your sewing machine has not been used for a while, it is a good idea to test that it is stitching correctly by sewing a seam with the presser foot on. If the tensions are correct and it is forming stitches properly, you will know that any problems encountered with free embroidery do not arise from a basic fault with the machine.

To prepare the machine for embroidery, remove the presser foot. This usually keeps the fabric flat on the bed of the machine and the embroidery hoop acts as a substitute for it. Without it you have a clearer view of the area you are embroidering. Lower the feed dog. This is usually done with a knob or a switch on the machine – consult the manual if you are unsure; it can be the same setting as for darning. If you are unable to lower the feed dog, the machine may have a raised plate to cover it. Alternatively, set the length of stitch on 0 so that the feed just goes up and down; this can interfere less with the freedom of movement than a raised plate does.

With the feed lowered, you are now in control of the length of stitch, governed by the speed the hoop is moved under the needle. The faster you move the hoop, the longer the stitch; the slower you move it, the shorter the length of stitch.

Try to have the machine running quickly and consistently. If the needle is moving quickly in and out of the work, there is less likelihood of breaking it because it will not be in the fabric as you are moving it.

Starting to embroider

Thread the machine with machine embroidery threads, using a different colour in the bobbin from in the top. This will enable you to see how different tensions affect the stitches.

Stretch some medium to lightweight fabric in the hoop, as described earlier, with right side uppermost. Place the hoop under the needle and lower the presser bar. It is easy to forget this, as the foot is no longer there, but it is essential because it is this action that engages the top tension. Without any top tension, the flow of thread is unrestricted and can cause considerable knotting on the reverse side of the work or around the bobbin case. If this happens, carefully cut all the threads away, taking care not to cut the embroidery. Clean away all the threads from around the bobbin case and start again.

Pull the bobbin thread through the fabric by holding the top thread and turning the wheel by hand. Hold both threads to prevent any knotting underneath. Keep your fingers on the embroidery hoop; this helps your control and it is a safe place for them. Make sure that you are comfortable, that the needle is in line with your nose and that you are at the correct height to sew. When beginning to embroider, you may feel rather tense and later suffer with neck or backache, so do try to be comfortable and relaxed before you start. To give yourself good control of the hoop, try resting one elbow or a forearm against the table. This gives a pivot point and can make moving the hoop easier.

Holding the two threads, make a few stitches and cut off the tails; you are now ready to proceed. You are free to move the hoop in any direction at any speed and in any type of movement you desire. It does not matter whether the machine is set on zigzag or running stitch: you are not restricted to moving in any one direction. You must, however, keep the hoop flat on the bed of the machine.

Try to keep the hand movements smooth and the speed of the machine consistent. When you start to embroider, you may encounter some of the following problems:

1 *The fabric puckers in the hoop.*
This could be caused by the thread tensions being too tight or the fabric not being taut enough in the hoop.

2 *The machine misses stitches.*
This could be caused by the fabric not being taut enough in the hoop or the needle being the wrong way around.

3 *Threads keep breaking.*
This could be caused by the threads being too thin or weak, or the fabric not being taut in the hoop.

4 *Needles keep breaking.*
This could be caused by moving the hoop too quickly or running the machine too slowly, which will bend, then break, the needle, or the top tension may be too tight.

If the machine will not sew properly when you are doing free embroidery, always check that the basics are correct: that the machine is threaded up correctly, the bobbin is in the right way around, the presser bar is down, and the needle is in correctly. These are often the cause. Going through a simple check-list is a logical way of discovering the problem.

When you want to remove the work from under the machine, move the needle to its highest position, lift the presser bar and, by turning the wheel by hand, release enough thread to enable you to slide the hoop from under the needle without putting any strain on thread or needle. If you pull the hoop out without doing this, you could bend the needle which will then break when you begin to sew again.

38

87

When experimenting with the techniques described, remember that there is not necessarily any 'right' or 'wrong' effect or texture. All types are relevant if appropriate for your subject matter; variety is the objective. Try to build up a collection of samples of these techniques and as many variations on them as you can produce. It will help you to practise and gain control, and will provide you with a catalogue of textures and techniques to refer to. Make simple notes how each was achieved: for example, types of thread, tension and type and speed of hand movements.

Straight stitch
Experiment with the machine set at straight stitch. Try to keep the speed of the machine fast and consistent. Vary the speed at which you move the hoop and notice the difference in length of stitch, which you now control.

Vary the hand movements you make to create different textures. You may find you have more control moving the hoop backwards and forwards than from side to side; also, circular movements are generally easier performed anticlockwise if you are right-handed. Try sewing lots of parallel lines close together. When they lie in different directions, the threads catch the light and appear as two different shades (fig 38).

Small, circular hand movements produce a versatile texture, which is actually a lot of small stitches in various directions all catching the light to give different shades of one colour. This is useful for shading and merging one colour with another. Work densely or loosely for different effects (fig 39).

Short backwards and forwards hand movements of varying lengths, moving the hoop slowly, will give a texture suitable for grass (fig 40).

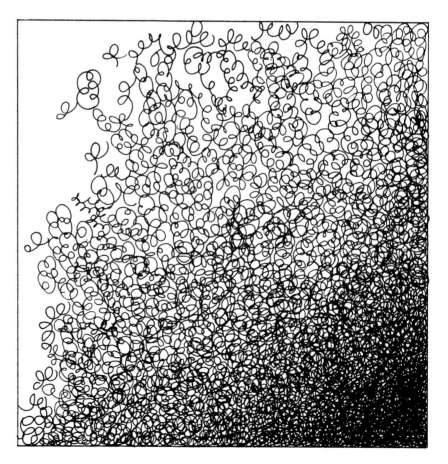

39

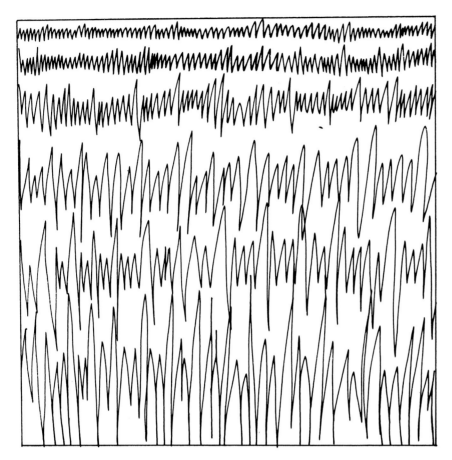

40

Experiment further and see how many textures and effects you can create with straight stitch.

Zigzag

Everything you have tried with running stitch can be done with the machine set on zigzag. The various speeds at which you move the hoop to vary the length of stitch will be more apparent with this stitch.

Try moving the hoop very slowly to achieve a solid satin stitch; moving the hoop a little faster will open this out. This is very useful for shading or for reflections in water.

You need a slow hand movement for a short stitch length. Row upon row of zigzag gives a solid, filling-in stitch. Note the tonal changes achieved with different directions.

By holding the hoop still and making several stitches on the spot, you can create the machine embroidery equivalent to french knots. Vary the widths and directions of stitch; this is a useful technique for flowers.

Moving the hoop from side to side will quickly fill large areas that need texture with a horizontal feel to them (fig 44).

Try moving the hoop with one hand and altering the width of zigzag with the other. Move the hoop slowly for a closely-worked satin stitch, going from the widest zigzag down to a running stitch you can draw with a line of varying width to create leaves, stems, branches, etc (figs 45a–d).

A machine with a stitch-width control that slides or turns easily is better than one which has a series of buttons for various set widths, which will give you steps rather than a smooth increase in width.

The marks made by zigzag are generally bolder and larger than those made by straight stitch, and are therefore more useful in the foreground of a picture.

The ivy archway

left The detail of the grass path is painted with care. The resist is used for guidelines within the flower border and to help with the perspective on the brick work

below, left The dark green trees in the distance are embroidered in a small running stitch worked in a circular motion to give an overall texture. A running stitch is also used for the dark tones amongst the flowerbed. A horizontal running stitch in brown is used for the soil

below, right The small area of brick wall bordering the flowerbed is worked in grey running stitches following the lines of perspective. Flowers of various colours are analysed and worked in running stitch or zigzag following the contour of each group. The cream in the ivy leaves is filled in with running stitch

opposite A light green is embroidered between the flowers. A yellow and light green are added to the ivy. Three shades of brown are used for the bricks. A light grey in the bobbin, with a loosened tension, is used to give a flecked appearance to the brown. Finally, an off-white running stitch is used to represent the mortar between the bricks

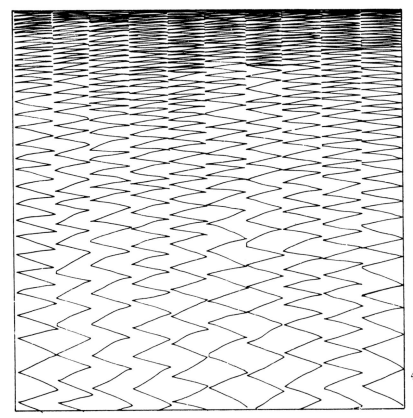

41 Opening out a zigzag is useful
for shading or for reflections
in water

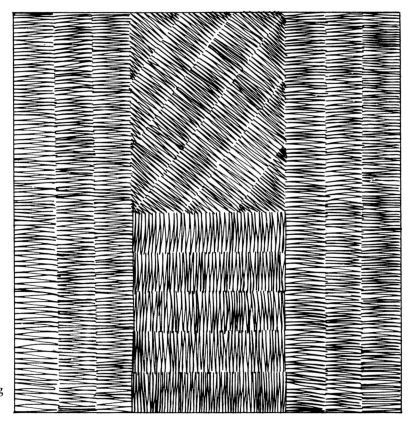

42 Tonal changes achieved by zigzag
in different directions

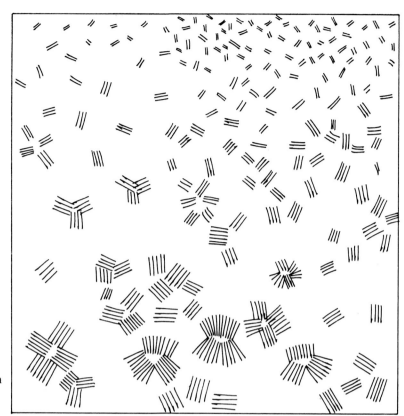

43 Varying the width and direction of the stitch is a useful technique for flowers

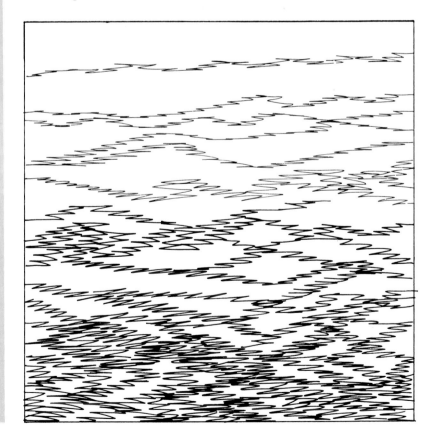

44

45a

45b

45c

45d

Altering the tensions

This will increase the variety of textures you can produce. All the suggested techniques for straight stitch and zigzag should be tried with altered tensions.

The bobbin tension

This is controlled by the tension screw on the tension band of the bobbin case. The screw on the end of the band holds it to the case, while the screw in the centre regulates the flow of thread. Turn the screw clockwise to tighten the tension and anti-clockwise to loosen it. Be cautious, as this screw is only approximately 3 mm (⅛ in) long. To enable you to revert to normal tension, remember how much you have turned the screw. Always try to achieve the effect you want with as little alteration as possible.

Even if your machine does not have a removable bobbin case, you can still alter the tension screw. Refer to the instruction book. You can also bypass the tension band, or remove it for a very loose tension or for using thicker thread.

Top tension

This is regulated by a control dial or wheel on the front or top of the machine. Consult the manual if you are unsure. If there are numbers on the control, the higher the number it is set at, the tighter the tension on the thread becomes; the lower the number, the looser it becomes. On some machines there is a window with a + and − sign. If the + sign shows, the tension is tighter; if the − sign shows, it is looser.

By combining different tensions on the machine, new textures and techniques are created. Experiment with the following ideas.

46 Whip stitch used for flowers

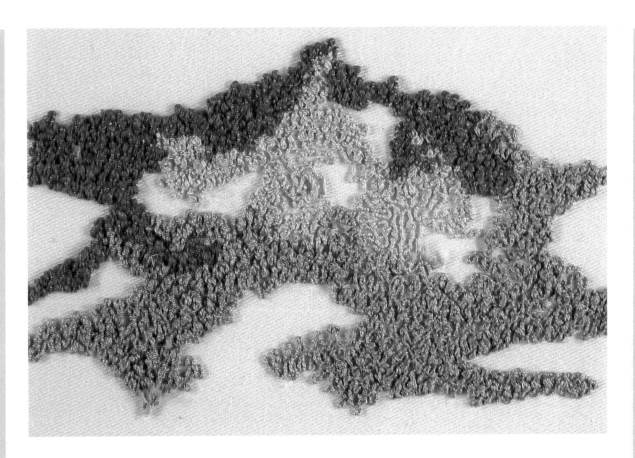

47 Moss stitch

Whip stitch

With the top tension tighter than normal and the bobbin tension looser, set the machine on running stitch and move the hoop in small spiralling or circular movements. This will give you whip stitch. By moving the hoop very slowly, the bobbin thread will appear to couch down the top thread; if moved more quickly and in circles, the bobbin thread creates a characteristic feathering effect. Working with a different colour in the bobbin from in the top will make it clear how this stitch is formed (by pulling the loose bobbin thread to the right side of the embroidery with the tight top thread).

Moss stitch

This technique uses the same altered tensions as whip stitch. Use a tight top tension and loose bobbin tension, with the machine set on straight stitch. Hand wind stranded cotton, perlé, crewel wool or tapestry cotton on to the bobbin. Thread up the top of the machine with ordinary machine embroidery thread. To get the tension loose enough for this technique to work, you may need to bypass or even remove the tension band on the bobbin case.

This stitch is worked with the right side of the embroidery face down, so the outline of the shape to be filled in with moss stitch should be marked in with a running stitch on the machine before you take the work out of the hoop and restretch it face down. Pull the thicker thread through to the top to hold, in order to prevent knotting. This thread then remains out of sight on the right side of the embroidery for the rest of the technique.

Move the hoop in small backward and forward movements to create the characteristic knobbly, towelling type texture. Moss stitch gives a bold texture suitable for foliage

The garden at White Rock

above The background for the composition shown in Fig 55a

opposite, top All the dark tones in the foliage are embroidered in running stitch. The brick wall is embroidered with running stitches to represent the mortar

opposite, below The flowerheads are embroidered mostly in small zigzag stitches. The leaves on the hosta in the foreground are highlighted in running stitch

overleaf Mid green and then light green are used for the foliage amongst the flowers and the tree, worked in a running stitch following the direction of growth

The garden at White Rock:
the finished embroidery

on trees, bushes, shrubs or gravel. Worked in a straight line, in straight stitch, the thicker thread appears couched down, which provides a strong outline within a composition, or would be suitable for foreground grasses.

If you are going to use this method a lot on a piece of embroidery, complete the moss stitch areas first so that you can then re-stretch your fabric the right side up and continue the embroidery, incorporating the moss stitch with the rest of the stitching.

Bold surface decoration

Couching threads

Any thread too thick or unsuitable to hand wind on to the bobbin can still be used by being couched down with a zigzag stitch using normal tension, top and bobbin, and machine embroidery threads. Several types of thread can be couched, for example, wool, rafia, perlé and mohair. They can be mixed colours, laid down flat, or twisted together in straight lines or randomly. They could be used to outline shapes or fill in large areas quickly and boldly with lots of texture. Threads can be looped and anchored down at intervals, creating an effect like carpet pile which could either be cut or left as loops. The colour of the threads used to couch can either blend in or contrast. If piping cord is laid down and covered with zigzag, it is very effective for tree trunks or branches, depending on the scale of work.

Appliqué

This is a useful technique to achieve a block of colour in a composition which does not require the texture that stitches would give. The processes described here also apply to

48 Moss stitch

102

the section on collage. When applying one fabric to another the grain lines (warp and weft threads) should match, to avoid puckering and distortion.

There are two basic types of appliqué. The first is a practical method which gives a neat sharp outline of zigzag stitch. This is achieved by cutting the required shape out of fabric in a similar weight to the background, with a 1.5 cm (½ in) allowance all round. This is pinned to the background fabric and sewn down with a straight stitch 1.5 cm (½ in) in from the raw edge. The excess fabric is cut away and the edge is neatened with a zigzag stitch wide enough to cover the running stitch and the raw edge. If this is done with the fabric stretched in a hoop, intricate shapes can be appliquéd. The hoop must be moved slowly for a closely worked stitch.

The second type of appliqué actually merges one fabric with another, rather than creating a feature of the join. For this to work successfully the threads used in the top and bobbin of the machine must match the fabric. The piece is cut to the required size and sewn down with a straight stitch just inside the raw edge. With the machine set on straight stitch, make slow circular hand movements as shown in Fig 39. This should be worked in an irregular shaped band covering the raw edge and extending on to the background fabric. This is a useful technique if you want the stitches to merge with fabric, rather than stand out boldly as they would with zigzag.

Quilting

This is a technique which will give raised padded areas to an embroidery. There are

49 Appliqué merging one fabric with another, combined with English quilting

various types of quilting, all of which are versatile and offer a lot of potential when used in conjunction with embroidery. Quilting can be worked either in or out of a hoop. As a general rule, smaller intricate shapes are easier to follow with the work in a hoop while large areas with predominantly straight lines are easier with the presser foot on.

English quilting

The basis of English quilting is sewing through three layers of fabric to give an all-over effect, with the fabric raised between the stitches. A firm backing fabric, an inner layer of wadding and a top layer should be tacked together by hand to avoid them slipping. If this is put in a hoop, make sure all three layers are stretched tight – this will flatten the wadding completely, but do not worry: it will spring back when removed from the hoop. This type of quilting can be done at the same time as the embroidery, but if you want an area to be embroidered with detail and yet be a raised part of the quilting, the embroidery must be executed before the wadding and backing fabric are added. If the work is heavily embroidered at the quilting stage, that area will be flat, and only the areas without embroidery will be raised.

Trapunto

This is used for padding small selected areas in a composition. Two layers are used. The top fabric should be lightweight and pliable and the backing fabric firm, otherwise the padding will be more prominent on the reverse side. The shape should be outlined in straight stitch. Slit the backing fabric and push in a quantity of kapok or wadding. Oversew the slit together by hand. This technique is useful for padding isolated shapes, perhaps in the foreground for added depth or for increasing interest in the focal point. It is ideal for representing rocks or pebbles.

Italian quilting

This is in the form of raised channels, and is suitable for strong outlines in a picture, such as the lines of a ploughed field, tree trunks or branches, or, on a larger scale, flower stems or stamens.

It is created by straight stitch with a twin needle, or two parallel rows of straight stitch worked with a single needle. These are sewn through two layers of material. The bottom layer must be of an open weave, such as muslin. The channels are sewn and then wool is threaded through them to form the padding. A blunt quilting needle is used, and should be taken in and out of the muslin if the channel is long or curved.

Creative lace

This is a method of creating features or motifs in a lace technique. You can produce abstract shapes, leaves, trees or spider's webs, to lay over the composition. These features are made independently of the picture and stand out more when in place than similar features embroidered directly on to the work. It is possible to mount trees 1–2 cm (½–¾ in) proud of the embroidery, using a box frame to achieve a sense of depth.

Shapes to be applied to an embroidery may benefit from a coating of spray starch to keep their construction rigid. They should be hand sewn in place, requiring only a few stitches to hold them.

Lace work

Stretch a medium-weight fabric, something that does not fray easily, in the embroidery hoop. Use machinery embroidery thread No. 30 or a polyester and cotton mixture, as these are less likely to break. Set the tensions on the machine slightly tighter than normal. Outline a simple shape, a circle or rectangle, in running stitch. Cut out the fabric inside the stitch line, then restretch the fabric in the hoop. Straight stitches are worked across the hole, in various directions for an abstract

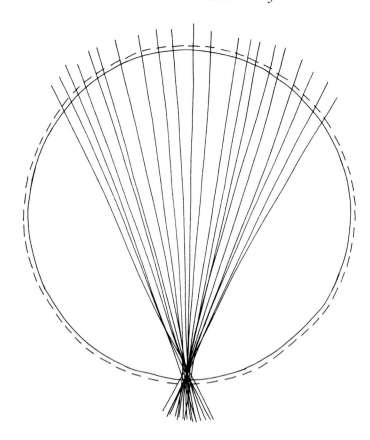

50 Running stitches are worked across the hole cut in the fabric. Stitch at least 1.5 cm (½ in) on to the fabric

51 The first 3 cm (1 in) of running stitches at the base of the design are gathered loosely with the widest zigzag to form the tree trunk. More running stitches are added at this point. Do not work the zigzag too densely at this stage, otherwise it becomes too thick to stitch into

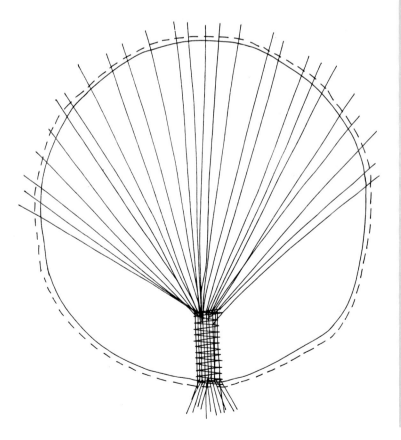

The avenue

left The painted background

below, left The most distant area is worked first in diagonal running stitch to echo the shafts of light coming through the trees. The dark foliage immediately above it can then be embroidered as branches overlap the area. The light foliage towards the top of the composition is then worked in a small whip stitch before the branches can be embroidered. Some distant branches and tree trunks are worked in running stitch. The distant part of the pathway is worked in a small whip stitch in a horizontal direction

below, right Working towards the foreground, lighter tones are used for the foliage, tree trunks and the pathway using the same techniques as above

opposite In the foreground, closely worked zigzag is used for the branches and tree trunks and zigzag worked on the spot for the larger leaves. This is a bolder mark than running stitch and makes the features stand out more, giving depth to the picture

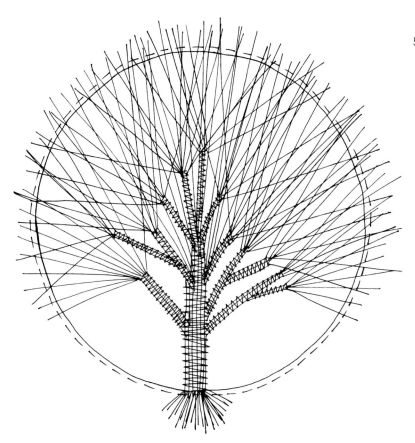

52 Loosely bind together more of the running stitches higher up the tree shape with a slightly narrower zigzag. Add more running stitches from these points to the outer edge

53 Bind together the running stitches toward the top of the tree with narrow zigzag. Add more running stitches if necessary. Only a few lines of narrow zigzag should go as far as the outer edge. When satisfied with the shape, work over all the tree again with a closely-worked zigzag to neaten and thicken where necessary. This could have a simple collage or painted landscape placed behind it and be framed with a circular mount. Alternatively, cut out the tree, spray with starch and hand stitch into position on an embroidered composition.

design, or to form the basis of a tree shape or of whatever design you require. These threads can then be thickened by working over them with zigzag. If the machine is set on a wide zigzag, many of the threads will be gathered together. Either work over them randomly or gather them in an organised fashion to form a distinctive shape.

When sewing across the hole, keep the movement of the hoop slow and consistent, especially if you want a closely-worked satin stitch to bind the straight stitches neatly. You can build up a considerable thickness by working over the zigzag several times. When completed, the shape can be cut away from the fabric. If it is a complex shape that needs fabric around it to keep the structure intact, it may be possible to cut some fabric away and hide the remainder under the card mount which will frame the finished embroidery.

Soluble fabrics

The size of the hole you can cut out and sew across within a hoop restricts the size of the embroidered motif you can make with the lace technique. Sometimes there is also the restriction of the fabric holding the construction together. To make embroidered lace motifs on a larger scale and with fewer constraints, it is often better to use soluble fabrics. These have the advantage of providing a surface on which to draw out the design to act as a guide. The design can be as large as required because the hoop can be moved to complete the embroidery. As with lace work, a good construction with running stitches is essential, when creating a shape, otherwise when the fabric is removed the work will fall apart. Start with a basis of straight stitches and thicken these with zigzag where appropriate.

54 Cut a rectangle in the fabric and work groups of running stitches to form the basis for a row of trees

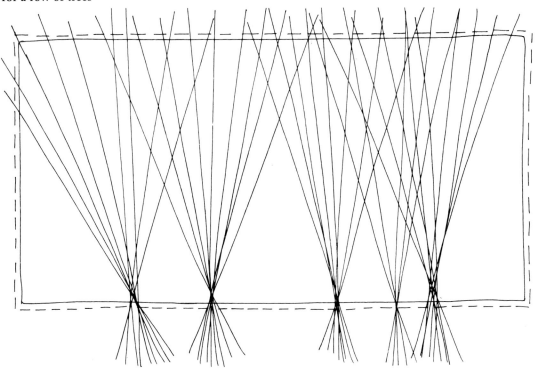

55 A lace-work tree laid
over a collage

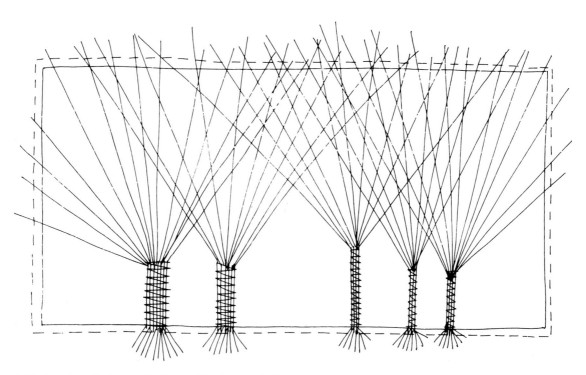

56 Gather the stitches at the base with zigzag stitch

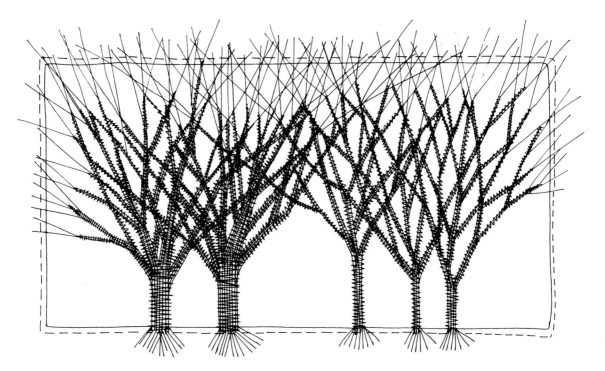

57 Continue to work as for Figs 44 to 47

There are four different types of soluble fabric suitable to use with this technique.

Acetate fabric

This is stretched in the hoop, embroidered over and then dissolved in acetone. It is a rather messy option.

Vanishing muslin

This is like ordinary bleached muslin in appearance, but needs care when being stretched in the hoop, as it is a brittle material which will tear easily. Once the embroidery is completed the work is pressed with a hot iron until the muslin turns dark brown. It will then crumble away from the embroidery. This can take quite a long time, and if the embroidery is very thick in some areas it is difficult to get the iron to touch the muslin. Also, the dust and mess created by the muslin is unpleasant.

Cold-water-soluble fabric

This is a plastic-like material which also requires care when being stretched in the hoop, as it is delicate in nature. Sew on it slowly and carefully otherwise it will tear. The advantage of this material is the ease with which it dissolves in cold water. Use a pencil for marking out the design, as any waterbased marker will dissolve the fabric. When the embroidery is complete, pin out the shape on a polystyrene tile before dissolving the fabric.

Hot-water-soluble fabric

This is a strong, woven, lightweight fabric, which is the easiest of the four to work with. It will stretch in the hoop like ordinary fabric and you can use any marker to draw on it. When the embroidery is complete, pin out the shape on a polystyrene tile as for the cold water fabric, this helps to keep the shape of the construction. Place it in a sink or bowl and pour hot water over it until all the fabric has dissolved. Leave pinned in place until dry.

The water garden

left The painted background

below, left Two shades of dark green are embroidered in running stitch in the direction of the growth of the foliage and trees. The leaves in the foreground are drawn in zigzag.

opposite The flowers in the distance are embroidered in running stitch and zigzag. A mid tone of green is added to the tree and in between the flowers in the distance. The handrail on the bridge is embroidered with zigzag. More leaves in the foreground are drawn in zigzag in a lighter tone of green. The burgundy flower stems in the foreground are embroidered in a very narrow zigzag and a running stitch. A light green is added in running stitch between the flowers in the distance to soften their appearance. The final shade of green is embroidered on the tree to give it depth and solidity. The pink flowerheads in the foreground are worked in a small zigzag with a sideways motion. The foreground leaves are embroidered in parallel rows of running stitch or drawn in zigzag

below, right A detail of the foreground

6

TRANSLATING A PHOTOGRAPH INTO STITCHES

Whilst working on an embroidery I keep its original photographs by my side to refer to. I analyse each area in terms of colour and the type of stitch needed to achieve certain textures and effects. I automatically see textures within a picture as stitches, which is a result of a lot of experimenting and practice over the last ten years. This way of working condenses several processes into one.

A good interim stage is to make a simple pencil sketch or tracing of the composition. Taking different areas one at a time, try to see them as the types of mark you would make with a pencil to represent them. These marks can then be seen as stitches; you must decide what size they should be, how many and which direction they should follow. As a general rule, if looking at an open landscape of grass or moorland, the area just below the horizon can be seen as a series of fine, closely drawn horizontal lines which gradually open into the middle distance. Further forward, these horizontal lines are made up of short, vertical strokes of the pencil, while in the foreground the grasses become stronger vertical and diagonal lines of varying thicknesses (fig 59).

Analyse the photograph. First of all, a decision should be made between texture and non-texture. Select features without texture which can be left painted to help balance the composition in terms of busy and quiet areas.

The next stage is to decide on the types of texture or stitch which best describe certain elements. If an area requires stitches for emphasis but does not have much texture, it could be best filled in with straight stitch, worked in lines, close together; for example, worked horizontally to describe a flat road, field, lawn or still water. Follow the contours of a shape such as a rock in the foreground or

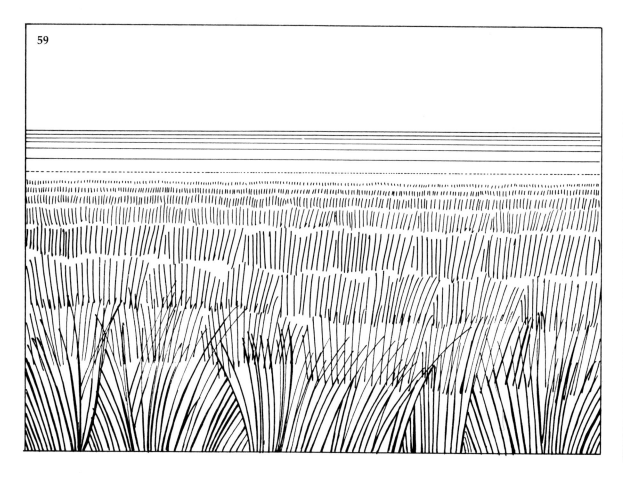

59

mountains in the distance in straight stitch. With any type of stitch, this often helps make a feature look three-dimensional.

The stitches or marks have a direction to follow. There is often a linear feel to things. A tree may appear to lack direction within its foliage until closer analysis reveals a strong diagonal sweep to the leaves along the branches; the direction changes depending on the type of tree. Flowers, for example, may seem to grow in a disorganised group, but the heads all face the same way, indicating the direction of mark to make.

The scale of the marks or stitches you make will be determined by where in the composition a feature is placed. Larger, bolder marks are generally found in the foreground.

60a *An autumn lane*

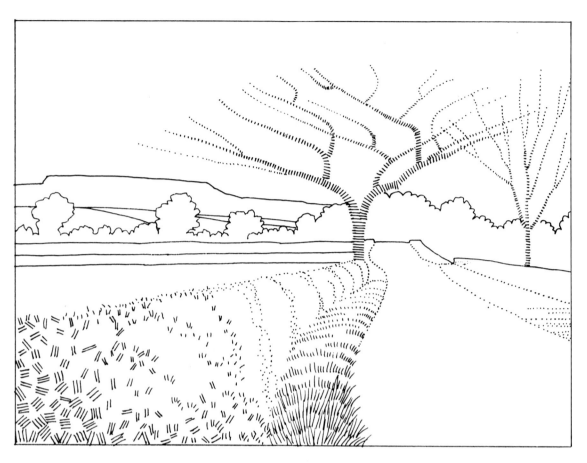

60b This is an analysis of a photograph in terms of
marks made with a pencil. Areas such as the
road, sky, fields and mountain in the distance
are best left as painted areas because of their
lack of texture. They serve as a contrast to the
busy areas in the composition

60c The hedge is seen as a group of randomly-placed marks, larger ones in the foreground to be interpreted as various widths of zigzag worked on the spot. These become smaller in the distance, eventually changing to straight stitch worked randomly but following the contours of the hedge

60d The grass verge is seen as a series of horizontal lines in the distance, becoming short vertical lines in horizontal bands further forward. In the foreground these get longer and overlap the previous row. This would be embroidered in straight stitch

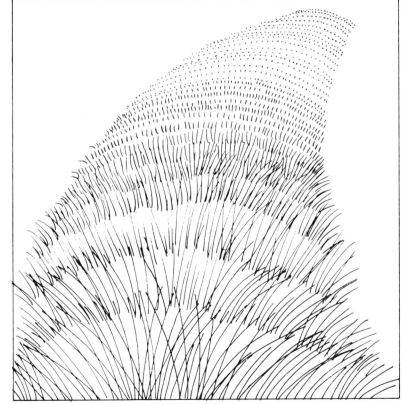

60e The trees are lines of varying thickness, ideally drawn with a closely-worked zigzag, which tapers down to a straight stitch

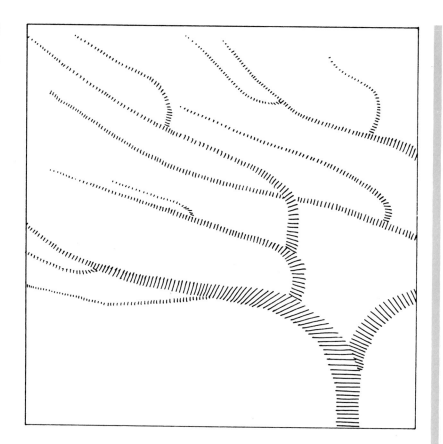

60f The trees and bushes in the distance are made up of small marks all lying in different directions creating a subtle texture. This could be interpreted with small circular movements in running stitch, like whip stitch, worked more densely at the base of the shape

61a *The garden at White Rock*

An autumn scene

left The position of the small trees in the distance is marked in with the line of resist. Some detail is painted in, this helps at the embroidery stage with the selection of colours and direction of stitch

below, left The tree trunks are drawn in zigzag or running stich. The distant foliage is embroidered in khaki green in small running stitches. Two shades of yellow are embroidered in the foliage at this stage so other colours embroidered on top will break up the yellow stitches

below, right More tree trunks and branches are added. The foliage has a diagonal feel to it. It is embroidered with a small whip stitch following this direction. The fallen leaves are worked in the same technique in a horizontal direction

opposite More colours are added to the foliage. A few leaves are embroidered with a zigzag worked on the spot in front of the tree on the right. These help give depth to the picture

61b A garden scene with a great variety of textures and stitches to analyse. The sky and lawn are seen as flat colour and the wall is only lightly textured. These provide areas of calm to balance the busy flower border full of texture and colour

61c The groups of flowers are seen as marks lying in the same direction, depicted as various widths of zigzag worked on the spot, becoming larger in the foreground

61d The shape of the leaves of the phlox in the foreground can be seen clearly. These could be worked in a varying width of zigzag, from the narrowest width to the widest and back again. The flower head is depicted as a group of small dots, interpreted in stitch as a narrow zigzag

61e The wall is seen as a flat colour with broken vertical and horizontal lines following the lines of perspective. These would be embroidered in straight stitch and the painted silk would represent the bricks

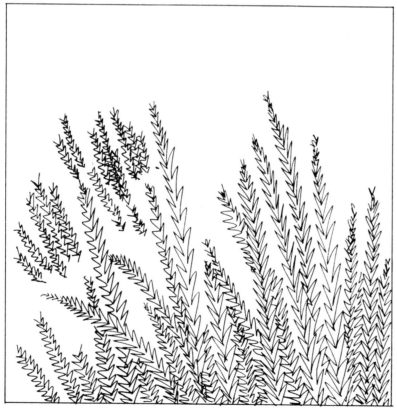

61f Various areas of foliage could be represented by texture with a vertical sense of direction. Worked as a running stitch in a short backwards and forwards movement

61g The achillea is
depicted as fine
vertical lines with
short, wider,
horizontal lines.
These could be
interpreted as
vertical running
stitches with wide
blocks of zigzag on
top

61h Daises, which are
large enough in the
composition for
individual petals to
be seen. These are
embroidered with a
closely worked
zigzag, fanning out
to form the shape of
the flower

7
STARTING TO EMBROIDER A PICTURE

62 Sort threads into colours

You need to be organised when beginning to work on an embroidery. Surround yourself with all the relevant photographs, design sketches, analysis of textures in the form of notes or sketches and any samples of stitches you may find relevant. With the aid of the photographs and the collage or painted background, choose all the threads the picture will need. For each area to be embroidered, decisions must be made in terms of colour, texture and technique to be used. When you have selected the 'palette' of colours, make notes on the design sketch showing which colours to put where.

You will need to break down the number of colours needed in one area; also the various shades which, when combined in stitch, recreate in embroidery the feature in the photograph.

There are several ways to mix colours in stitch. For example, you can use one colour in the bobbin and another on the top of the machine, with the top tension tighter than normal, to bring up the bobbin thread enough for it to show; or loosely embroidered areas in one colour, with another colour stitched on top, so both can be seen; or try combining colours in thread with the painted silk background showing between the stitches.

It is the combination of colours in stitch, used in the right proportions, and the texture in embroidery, which will create the effect you require.

I always start in the background or the most distant point of a picture. This is where I want the smallest stitches, palest, coolest colours and least texture to help create the depth I want. When larger-scale stitches and techniques are worked in the foreground, this first area will recede. Any area with branches or anything cutting across it must be worked first; this is generally a progres-

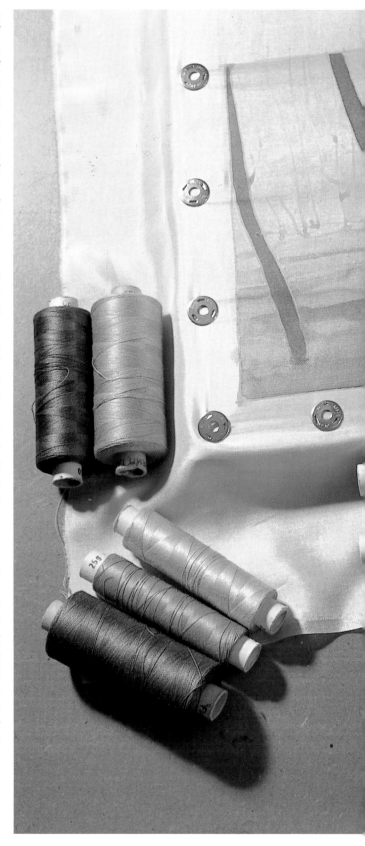

63 **Cottons selected ready to embroider the painted background. The composition is taken from one photograph, but the colours will be a combination of both**

64

sion from background to foreground.

When working toward the foreground, build up the scale of stitch and technique; the colours and tones should generally get stronger.

When embroidering an area requiring three or four shades of colour, start with the darkest and build up to the lightest. Do not work the stitches too densely if there are other colours to go on top, otherwise the area becomes too thick to stitch through, which will cause the thread to break and the machine to miss stitches.

Depending on the size of the embroidery, the scale of stitch could progress from straight stitch through zigzag, couching and moss stitch to quilted areas in the foreground.

Remember that the photographs are only a starting point. They provide the composition, colour and detail references you need, but do not have to be followed slavishly. They provide ideas, but the enthusiasm and inspiration for the subject matter comes from you and is the most important element. Walking in that landscape or garden and feeling the atmosphere, you can observe more than a camera can record. At some stage the photograph becomes obsolete and the embroidery starts to work in its own right, the colours working together within the embroidery rather than matching the photograph exactly. There has to be interpretation; an artistic style, rather than a photographic reproduction. Let the work develop beyond the starting point.

This medium gives all the scope that watercolour and oil painting does, plus much more: the possibilities are endless. Hence the fascination it holds, and the pleasure and excitement it gives. There is so much to learn and to experiment with, yet effective results can be achieved even at a beginner's level. It lends itself so well to landscapes and gardens because of its nature. The textures the machine stitch provides are appropriate to represent trees, leaves, grass and flowers on any scale.

Henry and Mary's garden

Quite a simple painted background. The composition is divided into four sections of colour, with the resist used to map out the positions of the flowers in the border

The dark tones are embroidered in running stitch, describing the direction of growth and type of texture in the foliage

A lighter tone of green is
added

A third, lighter green is
added to the background
trees. The flowerheads are
embroidered in a variety
of stitches, using zigzag
and running stitch. A running stitch in a circular
motion is used for the
pink poppies in the fore-
ground

Two shades of green are embroidered within the foliage, helping blend the flowers into the composition and aiding the sense of depth

SUPPLIERS

UK

Barnyarns
Old Pitt's Farm
Langrish
Petersfield
Hampshire
GU32 1RG
(general embroidery supplies,
fabric paints, fabrics)

Bernina Sewing Machines
Bogod House
50–52 Great Sutton Street
London
EC1V ODJ
(sewing machines)

Borovick Fabrics Ltd
16 Berwick Street
London
W1V 4HP
(fabrics)

Campden Needlecraft Centre
High Street
Chipping Campden
Gloucestershire
(general embroidery supplies)

Christine Riley
53 Barclay Street
Stonehaven
Kincardineshire
AB3 2AR
(general embroidery supplies)

Creative Crafts
11 The Square
Winchester
Hampshire
SO23 9ES
(general embroidery supplies,
books, fabric paints)

Elna Sewing Machines (GB) Ltd
180–182 Tottenham Court Road
London
W1P 9LE
(sewing machines)

Framecraft Miniatures Ltd
148–150 High Street
Aston
Birmingham
B6 4US
(frames)

**Frister & Rossman Sewing
Machines Ltd**
Mark Way
Swanley
Kent
BR8 8NQ
(sewing machines)

George Weill & Sons
18 Hanson Street
London
W1P 7DB
(fabrics)

Hepatica
82A Water Lane
Wilmslow
Cheshire
(general embroidery supplies)

John Lewis
Oxford Street
London W1
(general embroidery supplies)

Jones Sewing Machine Co Ltd
Shepley Street
Guide Bridge
Audenshaw
Manchester
M34 5JD
(sewing machines)

Liberty & Co
Regent Street
London W1
(fabrics)

MacCulloch & Wallis
25–26 Dering Street
London
W1R OBH
(fabrics)

Mary Allen
Wirksworth
Derbyshire
DE4 4BN
(general embroidery supplies)

Needle & Thread
80 High Street
Horsell
Woking
Surrey
(threads)

New Home Sewing Machine Co Ltd
Cromwell Road
Bredbury
Stockport
Cheshire
SK6 2SH
(sewing machines)

Pfaff
Pfaff House
East Street
Leeds
LS9 8EH
(sewing machines)

Shades at Mace & Nairn
89 Crane Street
Salisbury
Wiltshire
SP1 2PY
(general embroidery supplies)

Silken Strands
33 Linksway
Gatley
Cheadle
Cheshire
SK8 4LA
(threads)

Viking-Husqvama Ltd
PO Box 10
Oakley Road
Luton
LU4 9QW
(sewing machines)

Whaleys (Bradford) Ltd
Hams Court
Great Horton
Bradford
West Yorkshire
BD7 4EQ
(fabrics)

USA

Aardvark Adventure
Box 2449
Livermore
California 94550

American Handicrafts
2617 W Seventh Street
Fort Worth
Texas 76707
(mail order embroidery supplies)

Appleton Brothers of London
West Main Road
Little Compton
Rhode Island 02837

Economy Handicrafts
50–21 69th Street
Woodside
New York 11377
(mail order embroidery supplies)

Lew Wards
Elgin
Illinois 60120
(mail order embroidery supplies)

One Stitch at a Time
102A Main Street
PO Box 114

Peters Valley Craftsmen
Layton
New Jersey 07851
(mail order embroidery supplies)

The Counting House at the Hammock Shop
Box 155
Pawleys Island
South Carolina 29585
(mail order embroidery supplies)

The Thread Shed
307 Freeport Road
Pittsburgh
Pennsylvania 15215

The Hidden Village
215 Yale Avenue
Claremont
California 91711
(mail order embroidery supplies)

The Thread Connection
1020 East Carson Street
Pittsburgh
Pennsylvania 15203

Threadbenders
2260 Como Avenue
St Paul
Minnesota 55108

Canada

One Stitch at a Time
102A Main Street
PO Box 114
Picton
Ontario
KOK 2TO

The Silver Thimble Inc
64 Rebecca Street
Oakville
Ontario
L6K 1JZ

BOOK STOCKISTS

The complete range of Batsford embroidery books is available from:

B. H. Blackwell Ltd
50 Broad Street
Oxford
OX1 3BQ

Bridge Bookshop
7 Bridge Street
Bath
Avon
BA2 4AS

Campden Needlecraft Centre
High Street
Chipping Campden
Gloucestershire

Chosen Crafts
46 Winchcombe Street
Cheltenham
Gloucestershire
GL52 2ND

Creative Crafts
11 The Square
Winchester
Hampshire
SO23 9ES

Creative Craft & Needlework
18 High Street
Totnes
Devon

Embroidery Shop
51 William Street
Edinburgh
EH3 7LW

Frank Herring & Son Ltd
High West Street
Dorchester
Dorset
DT1 1UP

Lalla Thomas
413 Abergele Road
Old Colwyn
Colwyn Bay
Gwynedd

Ruskin's Bookshop
27 Bell Street
Romsey
Hampshire
SO51 8GY

Shades at Mace & Nairn
89 Crane Street
Salisbury
Wiltshire
SP1 2PY

Sutton Needlecraft Centre
40 Birmingham Road
Sutton Coldfield
West Midlands
B72 1QQ

The Embroiderer's Guild
Apartment 41
Hampton Court Palace
East Molesey
Surrey

The Handicraft Shop
47 Northgate
Canterbury
Kent
CT1 1BE

Voirrey Embroidery
Brimstage Hall
Brimstage
Wirral
Merseyside

Volumes
63 Queen Street
Glasgow

W. & G. Foyle Ltd
121 Charing Cross Road
London
WC2 OEB

Waterstone & Co Ltd
88–90 The Promenade
Cheltenham
Gloucestershire
GL50 1NB

Waterstone & Co Ltd
17 Milsom Street
Bath
Avon

Well-Head Books (Mail order)
25 Hamilton Road
Salisbury
Wiltshire

INDEX